You Can Change the World

The Secret to Reach Success and Leave a Legacy in 3 Iterations

Soufiane Erraji

Legal Deposit: 2019 MO 0467

Copyright © Soufiane Erraji, 2019

All rights reserved, including the right of reproduction or transmission in whole or in part in any form or by any means, electronic or mechanical, without express written permission from Soufiane Erraji.

soufiane.erraji.author@gmail.com

Preface

You Can Change the World is for all people who feel they can achieve more, who believe deep down that they can make an impact far greater than what they currently are up to, and who aspire to leave a legacy in all the areas they contribute to.

Through the story of Sarah, a promising young manager, and Mark, a part-time librarian & management guru, you will learn a time-tested method to achieve more, and stand out with head-turning results.

The examples illustrating the story come partly from real-life applications of the 3 Iterations method to Change the World.

As a management and personal development method, <u>You Can Change the World</u> will work best for you if you think of an immediate application while reading the book.

First Readers' Reviews

"The book is fantastic! The author's wisdom & fun nature shine through each page. I hope he writes many more!"

"The concept is powerful and refreshing because it reminds us that 1 person has the power to make so much change & so much good."

"I could not stop in the middle once I started; I loved the flow and the storytelling style."

"Insightful! I already identified areas where I will apply this powerful method."

"I liked a lot that the book offers a clear concept, concrete examples & summaries after each section. Thumbs up!"

"A book you'd love to read again and again."

Introduction

I have always been fascinated by accounts of individuals with a purpose, who achieve grand results and leave a positive impact on many around them; individuals who are not necessarily favored by wealth, power or extraordinary abilities or skills.

I have avidly read books about how exponential growth can be achieved, how ideas go viral, and was never fully satisfied, because none provided a specific method that I could follow to get there. Most accounts of success stories reinforced the luck component, the bet-the-bank type of risk, the unexpected intervention of some helping figure, the multiple failures needed before the one major success ...

If I overly simplify, what those books were screaming at me was "Believe in yourself! Go ahead! Dare to try! You might get lucky and succeed!". I don't know about you, but to me, it didn't sound motivating because I was looking for major success with smart risk taking, and possibly both smart and hard work.

The answer came to me from an unexpected source: my own experience! As I looked back on my 20-year career as an IT director at a Fortune 50 company, I identified a few examples of major achievements where I went far beyond my role to transform the way work was done, on a scale much larger than my natural area of responsibility.

As I examined each of these situations in detail, I noticed that I was following a pattern, starting with a grand vision of a better way of doing business, making it a reality in my circle of authority, so somehow flying below the radar, and then using that success as a working prototype to reapply at an exponentially higher level.

That was the inception of the 3 iterations method to change the world.

After the publication of this book, many readers of the 1st edition, from several countries, shared with me stories of how it worked for them too, how it inspired them to believe in their potential, gave them the practical step-by-step approach to achieve it, and how they applied it and obtained immediate results, whether at work, school, non-profit organizations, or in voluntary work for the benefit of the community.

So, I hope that you too will feel motivated to take action to achieve whatever vision you have for the world, starting from your immediate world, and then expanding to the larger one.

On the format of the book, I wanted it to be a short story, because that's how I personally learned the most. Books like "The One-minute manager", "Gung-Ho", "Who moved my cheese", to name a few, had the most impact on my younger self, so I adopted this format hoping to also maximize your appreciation of this book and the learning you take away from it.

Enough of this introduction, let the reading begin!

I wish you loads of brilliant successes!   *Soufiane Erraji*

Chapter 1

Sarah was a successful young production manager at the Innovative Consumer Chemicals Company, respected for her capabilities. The Plant where she worked had grown, under the direction of Plant Manager Ally, to become the company's largest elastomer manufacturing facility, with 30 production lines and 5000 employees. The finished products it manufactured were of high quality and shipped to customers all over the world. While the production process was relatively simple to describe, the demands of the job were high, as the lines ran at high speed and operated 24 hours a day, 6 days a week.

Every Monday, when the lines started up, it took about 30 minutes to reach the ideal temperature and pressure conditions, and at the end of every Saturday, the lines would slow down for 15 minutes until they came to a complete stop. All products manufactured early Monday and late Saturday were scrapped because they were below target quality standards. For the rest of the week, production managers and their teams worked hard to ensure continuity of operations and avoid any unplanned downtime that would impact production volume down and result in additional losses associated with each start-and-stop event.

In this environment, Sarah had a strong track record of meeting and sometimes even exceeding expectations. She had recently been promoted to her current position, becoming the youngest production manager in the company's history.

Everyone looked at her as a brilliant professional, and yet she felt that something important was missing.

She was sure she could do much more, more than just delivering what was expected of her. So, every year, she asked for more work and more responsibilities; each scope increase helped her slightly, but she was still not fulfilled.

She found many books on productivity, time management, effectiveness tips. She tried most of their recommendations, and yet, she still felt an inner sense of under-accomplishment.

One day, she went to the local library to continue her search. As she roamed through the aisles, she came across an old librarian, with a "How Can I Help You?" sign on his chest.

Sarah approached the man, who looked like a gentle, friendly grandpa. He seemed sympathetic and welcoming.

"Sir, can you guide me maybe?

- Of course, which book section are you looking for?

- Well, I am not so sure, possibly the personal or professional development aisle. Here is the situation: I am doing okay personally and professionally, and yet I feel I can achieve much, much more. I have been looking for resources to transform the situation, but none of the books I found, nor courses I took, met my specific need.

- And how important is this for you?

- Good question! You know, while I have what I need, and I could go on pretty much as I am, I'm afraid that I am losing my time, and that in a few years I'll regret that I didn't reach my true potential.

- So, you're talking about a profound change in your results and contribution.

- Yes, exactly! I can no longer stand to be a good average person, with good average results and making just an average impact on the world.

- Interesting! If I may ask, which area of your life would you want to transform the most? Is it your results at work, or your contribution to your family or your community?

- Let me think, I'd love to increase my impact on all of these; but if I need to choose, I feel I should start from my work.

- Hmm ... I see ... I may have an unconventional solution for you ... Not a book, but a hands-on method that will require your commitment and hard work in the next few months, if not few years.

- Really? Yes please, what is it?

- There is a method to Change the World in 3 Iterations, where each iteration will make you grow and will help you deliver increasingly bigger results.

- Changing the World! That's awesome, and scary too, I must admit. Okay, what is this method?

- Wait, young lady ... not so fast! I have some homework for you.

- What! Are you kidding?" Seeing the librarian's serious look, she added: "Okay, I am hooked, what is it?

- First, I need to tell you that I work in this library on a part-time basis; I am only here on the first Friday of every month, so this homework is for next month.

- Okay, what shall I do?

- As you chose to start your growth journey at work, here is your homework, till next time we meet: Consider an important project you're currently working on. Ideally, it'd have a sizeable impact both internally on your organization, and on your external community. If you have more than one candidate, favor the project for which you have a higher degree of passion.

- Is that all?

- Not quite; here is your challenge: how could you redefine the scope of the project in a way that stretches its expected deliverables and makes them truly exceptional without needing to ask for additional resources? Once achieved, these new deliverables should have the potential to be noticed by your hierarchy, praised in your company's internal communications, or featured in the local newspaper.

- That's a nice and vivid image indeed.

- Once done, here are 3 ways to further develop your inspirational vision:

1) Talk to a representative set of people who you expect will be positively impacted by your project and understand the impact it

has on their lives. This usually offers an eye-opening new perspective on the value and purpose of your work.

2) Identify ways to adjust the scope of your project to start benefiting twice as many people. These beneficiaries can come from within your company or from the external community if relevant.

3) Share your draft scope with each of the people who will be contributing to it and seek their inputs and improvement ideas.

By doing so, you will be able to improve your design, garner a lot of support for your transformation, and discover the first enabling habit of <u>Being in touch</u>.

- The first 2 points you mentioned are very new to me and I can't wait to implement them. Now, I've already gotten into the habit of involving my team members in the design of our initiatives, so I guess the last point won't benefit me much, right?

- I hear you. Do you listen to them as potential beneficiaries or mere contributors?

- Beneficiaries? How could they be so?

- There are many possible angles; your project could be helping them develop a specific skill, gain a certain experience, fulfill their craving for purpose and contribution, fill them with pride, enable their next career move, and so on. It's up to you to find out, through these 1-to-1 discussions. By committing to meeting these needs and expectations and including them in your project objectives, you strengthen the motivation of your entire team.

People naturally reject self-serving managers. And when they work for one, they tend to put in the minimum effort required. On the other hand, the more they feel supported, the more energy they put into work. In this sense, you get back as much as you invest in people and more.

- I am glad I asked this clarifying question! This makes perfect sense. It will take me 2 to 3 weeks to complete this exercise with quality, given that the list of people to meet will be quite long.

- So, do I understand that you are interested to embark on this journey?

- Definitely! I am feeling excited as I start to sense where this is going.

- I am glad to hear that.

- Then see you next month Mr. ... err... my name is Sarah by the way, what is yours, Sir?

- You can call me Mark.

- Then, see you next month, Mark."

Chapter 2

Sarah was puzzled by this encounter: within a few minutes this old man inspired her trust and made her confide in him!

She had shared her deepest thoughts of aspirations and self-doubt, which she seldom shared with anyone -let alone strangers- and yet, it felt natural for her to do so.

For some reason, that seemed perfectly okay! Was it the library environment, or how he slightly reminded her of her late grandfather, or was it because she felt he could read her like an open book?

Well, it does not matter; what he said made sense, and she was curious to find out how she would answer the homework, and more importantly, what these three iterations to change the world were!

The following days, Sarah thought hard about her worthwhile mission.

The old man had mentioned months if not years; so better choose one she had a passion for as he had wisely advised.

She finally opted for a recent waste recovery project aimed at reducing solid waste to landfill. Sarah's team had selected a third-party service provider who collected discarded products weekly and managed to recycle 70% of them. Although this allowed the factory to comply with local legislation, Sarah felt that it was not enough and that there could be a way to prevent 100% of this waste from going to landfill.

Following Mark's advice, Sarah asked her team members what they had liked most or least about that project and what they thought could have been done differently.

She was thrilled with the number of ideas she was getting. The interviewed colleagues mentioned their pride in having contributed to reducing the company's footprint, their satisfaction in having been able to hone their knowledge of legislation and their negotiation skills or simply to work on an original project very different from their work routine.

The most surprising and insightful comment came from the quality manager who mentioned that she had only reluctantly contributed to that project.

"Why is that?" Sarah asked.

"Don't get me wrong, the project is a massive improvement over our past practice. Still, I can't help but feel bad about all those well-functioning products that we throw in the trash, simply because they don't meet our exacting standards. I know this comment might sound weird, coming from a quality manager, but at the same time, I'm in a good position to know exactly what they're worth.

- Wait! That's a brilliant thought that completely changes the way we approach the problem."

Afterwards, Sarah thought long about that comment. Instead of asking what percentage of discarded products could be recycled, they should now be asking how these products could get a second life, or better yet, how could these products get a second life in a way that most benefits the local community.

This would help increase the number of beneficiaries, generate more pride for the employees participating in the project and contribute to the company's social responsibility objectives.

So, this slightly redesigned scope could open new unforeseen opportunities to deliver much more and multiply the impact of the project internally and externally.

It all seemed so obvious to Sarah now, and she was impatient to meet the old man to share her findings, and she couldn't wait to start acting on them!

The following Friday, Sarah went to the local library.

She was there before the opening and had to wait outside briefly in the cold morning. But that didn't matter to her; she was all in her thoughts, so she didn't notice a thing.

Five minutes later, she was in and literally rushed to the 'personal development' section, where Mark was already comfortably seated behind the counter.

"Oh, here you are! I'm glad to see you again.

- Hi Mark, I have a lot to tell you.

- I can easily tell!", he laughed. "Please come here and have a seat; it will be a long discussion, I guess.

- Actually, before I share my findings, I have a question for you.

- Yes, please?

- You had mentioned that the transformation is done in three steps.

- In three iterations, yes.

- Right, three iterations! And I don't see which these are in the homework you gave me.

- Oh! So, you think this is it? Not quite! Your homework is helping you to start unlocking the first iteration, which is to "**Master your Circle of Authority**".

To change the world, you will have to conquer two additional and larger Circles.

- Only the 1st one!

- Indeed. The overall method is simple to summarize, yet difficult to implement and takes many years to master:

These are three Iterations, enabled by three Habits, and maximized with three Personal traits.

Each Iteration builds on the success of the one before and extends its reach and impact manifold.

Put simply, in the 1st Iteration, you "**Master your Circle of Authority**" and deliver the best results and the maximum impact in your area of direct responsibility.

Here, most of the time, you don't need to seek permission, and the name of the game is smart envisioning and spotless execution.

Being in touch is the Habit that helps you to design right first time and avoid otherwise costly pitfalls.

Genuine care through Servant leadership helps you engage your people beyond simple obedience and gives you the spiritual motivation to pursue all of your bold goals.

- You are right! I could sense the difference firsthand over the past month.

All the above did materialize, and it is indeed filling me with a lot of excitement and energy to go that extra mile.

The insights I gathered are making it obvious to design new goals that double or triple current impact, with only slightly more effort.

- So, if you deliver what you have envisioned, where will this take you?

- I can already picture that article on the local newspaper and on the company internal billboard.

- Wonderful! So, go ahead, tell me what you found out and what your plans are before you start implementing over next month."

12

1ˢᵗ Iteration Instructions

- Choose a topic, possibly already in progress.
- Identify contributing people & beneficiaries.
- Be in touch with the contributing people: What's in it for them?
- Be in touch with the beneficiaries: How would their lives be improved?
- Try to double the list of beneficiaries.
- Adjust the topic target accordingly.
- Prepare a head-turning vision statement.
- Execute with excellence.
- Plan your communication.

14

Chapter 3

Sarah's vision was to partner with the local community to create new business opportunities for five to six young people, who would buy the discarded products at a nominal price and resell them locally for use under less stringent conditions and under a different brand name than ICCC's main product lines. This would allow full reuse of these items, while saving on recycling costs.

She shared this big idea with her team and was positively surprised at how easily she was able to share her enthusiasm with them.

After some thought, she realized that Being in touch also helped her connect the objectives to each team member's unique needs and wants, hence also unlocking their engagement.

In the same meeting, the team brainstormed to identify the work needed to enable that vision and suggested, among other things, developing new packaging and brand identity, adjusting logistics capabilities to be able to sell in smaller quantities compared to the usual full containers, launching the process of selecting thirty young people via a roadshow in local universities, and training them on the business best practices so that they can start vertically.

The list seemed daunting to Sarah who was concerned about the extra effort needed, but the room was buzzing with energy and passion, and there were at least two, if not three volunteers for each of the tasks at hand.

On top, given the importance of this project, Sarah was able to free up some capacity for the team by deprioritizing other work. In net it was a true "work smarter, not harder" situation.

Within three weeks, they made significant progress, five new businesses had been started and 80% of the scrapped products were already being resold.

Sarah presented this to Ally, her manager, who was impressed with so much accomplished so quickly and congratulated her on the significant community impact and the recycling cost savings that her small team had achieved.

"If only we could replicate this in the rest of my organization," she muttered.

So, it is with a lot of excitement that Sarah went to the next monthly meeting with her new mentor.

She found him in the same place and could hardly wait to bring about the good news:

"Hi Mark! It works! Your method works!

- I'm happy to hear it, and you know what? I'm not surprised, given your personal energy and how your vision had included components of hard business results, a meaningful contribution to the community, and genuine care for the well-being and success of the people in your team.

So, were you able to unlock their engagement and to bring them to the same level of excitement as yours?

- Yes! And that was maybe the biggest surprise!

I have literally discovered new facets of my team members, who clearly want to have a worthwhile and meaningful job, where they can contribute and be creative.

You know, once we started working, they suggested a few improvements to the plan that maximized our impact and optimized our efforts.

- **Congratulations** Sarah! And how about your management? What was their feedback?

- That is clearly another highlight of the past month! My manager couldn't believe it. She made me explain all of it at length: the vision, the plan, the results, the contribution of each member, the impact on the community ... and the draft newspaper article!

- So, there was a newspaper article after all?

- Yes, it will be published next week. Here is the draft that the reporter shared with me.

- Impressive results, Sarah! Well done.

- You know what, I feel that my manager too has discovered a new facet of me. I can see it in how she now seeks my opinion instead of giving me direct specific orders ... and I appreciate this change a lot.

- Excellent news ... I can tell you are ready now.

- Ready? For what?

- For the next iterations, remember?

- That's right! I realized that you hadn't yet shared much about the next two iterations, despite my direct question last month. I am sure you did it on purpose!

- Fair enough", he smiled. "I felt that it was important that you focus solely on Mastering your Circle of Authority, to be solidly grounded as we embark on the rest of the model.

- Okay, I'm ready for it.

- The method to Change the World in 3 Iterations is:

<u>1st Iteration</u>: **Master your Circle of Authority**

<u>2nd Iteration</u>: **Expand to your Circle of Belonging**

<u>3rd Iteration</u>: **Conquer 1+ Level Up**

- What is my Circle of Belonging?

- Now, you're no longer in your area of direct responsibility, you're venturing into, typically, your boss' Circle of Authority.

In this iteration, your scope is larger, and you replicate your initial success with your manager and your peers.

- How can I do that?

- Here, you can no longer rely on your sole authority. You embark your manager in your endeavor; you paint an image of success that encompasses them and your peers, and you invite them to join you in your undertaking.

- Wow, I am not sure I can do that.

- Equally to the first iteration, having a grand vision about the change at hand and its potential impact, internally and externally, will generate a lot of positive energy for you and others, so I strongly advise that this be the first step.

You will also need to gain or sharpen, additional skills and habits to enable you in this iteration.

Mind you, this iteration also applies to non-work-related changes, where you also grow your application environment by one level.

So, if you ran your 1st iteration with yourself or a group of close friends being your Circle of Authority, then your Circle of Belonging could be your larger family or all your social networks connections.

And if you ran your 1st iteration with your house as your Circle of Authority, then your Circle of Belonging for the 2nd iteration could be your street, your larger neighborhood, or your district."

20

Chapter 4

The Second iteration made sense to Sarah: it held a significant growth potential; so, she wanted to learn more about the enablers.

"Okay, I get it. What new skills and habits are needed in this iteration?

- As you need to collaborate with others on whom you have no authority, there are many possible enablers to help you do so. My preferred, by far, are Trust and Fun.

- Really? I was expecting communication skills or even negotiation; so, Trust and Fun are coming as a surprise, I admit.

- The first reflex when trying to have others to join you could indeed be to convince them with arguments or to look for a compromise to meet them in the middle. Building and maintaining Trust is much more profound, more powerful, and more sustainable.

- How do I then increase my trust in others?

- Please note I'm talking about Trust being established both ways. What I meant is that you should primarily establish yourself as a trustworthy person.

The people you seek to attract should trust your noble selfless intentions to join your quest. No negotiation or compromise will cover for the lack of Trust in the long run.

- So how can I get people to trust me?

- Being trustworthy is a personal trait you nurture for life, one interaction at a time.

To maximize it, consider communicating clearly and consistently about your intentions and your Motivations.

- Interesting. It makes sense now. So, if <u>Trust</u> is the supporting personal trait, how about <u>Fun</u> as the enabling habit?

Here again, if I usually bring some fun in my own team, I don't dare to do the same with my manager. At the contrary, I make sure to be fact-based and rather direct, to show how professional I am.

- A question, please: why do you bring fun within your team?

- Well, it makes our day more enjoyable, it reinforces our relationship, and for some people, it is more engaging to operate in a friendly environment instead of a formal one.

- Very well! And in what way are your peers different?

- I see where you're going. I still don't see why I should. We are talking about including my peers into changing our common Circle. Why would <u>Fun</u> be needed, and why more than other habits?

- I like how you are thoroughly thinking. I bet you're already picturing yourself with your colleagues, trying to embark them in your mission to Change the World.

- Somehow, yes.

- Well, look, to start this second iteration, you can leverage your recent success with the first iteration to get your boss to mandate that your peers work with you, or you can also directly preach your mission to them.

While both may be challenging, this is nothing compared to the subsequent effort to keep your colleagues motivated and engaged for the many following months if not years.

Experience shows that their engagement will fade with time, some sooner than others; and only a handful, if any at all, will stick around you because they too believe in the mission.

- Right! I can see that the task is more daunting than I pictured when you first talked about the second iteration. I wasn't sure I could get my colleagues' buy-in, and now I am scared with the full effort at hand!

- And here is where Fun becomes a key enabler.

While engaging the resources you need is a serious undertaking which should be done professionally, it is in your best interest to make the planning, the execution, and the ongoing progress tracking as light as possible and as enjoyable as possible.

- Or said differently: as Fun as possible!

- There you go! As Fun as possible indeed.

- Okay, okay ... let me think, I could literally picture the mission as a Quest, and its milestones as steps of that quest, where each completed step would lead to a trophy.

Yes, I can see how we could turn this into an engaging experience ... and for those who wouldn't buy into it from the start, I could design some complementary recognition system to celebrate significant achievements and if I can have some budget, I could plan for team building activities as well.

- Wow! My turn to be impressed! These are all great ideas, Sarah! Remind me, please: did I hear you say you were scared?

- Hahaha! You're doing magic, Mark.

- You are clearly already feeling the positive energy that this design generates, starting with you, and by extent, also for all the people who will join you.

There will be an effort needed at the start to properly design the Fun model, in a way that is uniquely linked to what your mission is, to the benefits you will deliver internally and externally and to your organization culture.

But this initial effort will be paid back manifold, in terms of engagement, speed and increase in the odds of delivering your mission.

- How do I make sure that the design of that Fun model is right? I guess that I can't change it once I declare it, right? So, how can I ensure that it is properly crafted?

- Great question! While you could apply some slight updates as you go -remember it could be a multi-year mission- it will indeed not be appropriate to significantly change it.

To maximize your chances of proper design, review your draft with a few people: first with some peers, then with representative of the people who will take part in your mission, and finally with all meaningful management.

And here I leave the interpretation of 'meaningful' to you, but these are all management-type people who may block your mission, totally or partially, if they disagree with your quest design.

Consider including them early on, immediately after having secured your boss' sponsorship; so, when you reach this point where you design your quest, these key people are already on your side and supportive.

- Genius! Mark, you are not a simple librarian, are you? Your method for me to Change the World in 3 Iterations isn't a theoretical one, right?

- Well, one can say I have had my lot of successes ... and failures too, to learn from. But we can talk about these later. So, what did we say so far?

- You said three Iterations, enabled by three Habits and maximized by three Personal character traits.

Each Iteration builds and expands on the success and the enablers of the previous one. And from what we discussed so far, each iteration starts with a carefully crafted vision that considers all possible contributions internally and externally, and by that, forces us out of our comfort zone and significantly expands our reach and impact.

I dare to say that each brings about exponential personal development and results both to our organization and to the communities we serve.

- Awesome statement, Sarah! And while we have not covered the third iteration yet, your statement is spot-on and perfectly summarizes the full method.

- Thank you! I have had a superb teacher.

- So, you were impatient to learn the method today. Do you want to go through the third iteration now?

- Well, I'd rather wait. I learned a lot today, and I'd like to apply your recommendations first, before going any further.

Last month, I grasped the benefit of focusing on one iteration before jumping to the next. So maybe we can cover it later once I progress enough on the 2nd iteration if you would agree? In the meantime, I will work on what I learned today as I already have many ideas to start with.

- This is a wise choice; I am very proud of my student!

As you rightly mentioned, the starting point for your second iteration is a well-crafted vision, and here again, leverage and expand the enablers you applied before, by thinking big on how you can serve others, and by <u>Being in touch</u> to tailor your mission to your new expanded audience.

- Thank you so much, Mark! I hope I will meet your expectations.

- Good luck my friend. See you next month then."

28

2nd Iteration Instructions

- Identify your Circle of Belonging.
- Expand your mission objective to this Circle.
- Adapt the head-turning vision statement.
- Secure needed sponsorship.
- Be in touch with the required contributors: What's in it for them?
- Declare your intentions to increase Trust.
- Plan some Fun: Gamification, Team building, Celebration, and Reward & Recognition.
- Execute with excellence.
- Plan your communication.

30

Chapter 5

A month later, Sarah met Mark again in the local library.

She had been busy building a coalition for her expanded mission. This time, she had quite a serious look on her face.

"Hi Sarah, good to see you again.

- Hi Mark, I've been looking forward to meeting you to share some observations and ask a few questions.

- Sure! What are these?

- Well, now that I started the second iteration, it opened my eyes to what can be done: I could make a difference for so many people, and what I am envisioning now could be reapplied across all the branches of the company where I work, and even beyond, to the entire industry. Now that I see this huge range of possibilities, I consider it to be my duty to contribute; not doing so would be such a waste!

- Great, that would be your third iteration, the one where you expand to one or more levels up ... I understand your impatience to go there but don't rush ... The second iteration is an important foundation for gaining skills and experience. While starting now to think about your grand vision for the 3rd iteration will give you a sense of urgency, I strongly recommend to remain focused on driving the second iteration to success.

- That's what I am doing, but I can't help to consider the range of possibilities.

- Well, tell me more about your renewed vision statement and about this past month's progress.

- As I report to the Plant manager, my Circle of belonging is all the site. My 2nd iteration is therefore targeting all 30 production lines, because all of them have a similar need to recycle the finished products manufactured during the start-and-stop events. Expanding my project to this scale will increase its impact 50 times, as most of the other lines are larger than mine. This is vertiginous growth, Mark! My usual way of doing things would have been to expand to other lines one at a time, and only if I have a solid relationship with the respective line manager. Now, I promised myself that I would follow your guidance to the letter and dare to shoot for my entire Circle of Belonging.

- And how did things go?

- Amazingly well! Engaging my peers was easier than I expected, thanks to my manager's sponsorship and to the newspaper article, which was published in the meantime.

- Really? How is that?

- Several colleagues felt inspired by the business results and the community contribution depicted in the article story and reached out to me proactively to offer their help, and some production managers even asked whether the project could be reapplied to their lines.

As a result, seeking their support for the expanded vision and gaining their initial willingness to join was much simpler than I had expected. Even a few members of the plant leadership council congratulated me and my team for our achievement.

- Okay. So, were all the people you needed equally easy to convince?

- No, not all of them; there were also some disbelievers. For instance, some commented that my team's initial success was linked to the small number of beneficiaries, and that expanding further with the same execution model would require a lot more efforts and be too costly.

- So, what have you done?

- Well, I learned from them and integrated their valid points into the design, and with this, I managed to turn them into supporters.

- That's brilliant!

- Well, it's thanks to something you said.

- Really? What is that, Sarah?

- I remembered that you said every iteration builds on the success and enablers of the previous one and expands it further.

- That's correct!

- So, I thought I'd continue building on the <u>Being in touch</u> skill which had enabled my 1st iteration. So, when I needed to include my peers in the expanded scope, I made a point to genuinely understand how they related to it, and how they could be positively impacted, all the while remaining open to any new learnings or change proposals that would make the concept even stronger.

- That's impressive! I am glad you captured the letter and the essence of my teaching.

- At this point, I was confident I had a solid concept, as it took all stakeholders' viewpoints in consideration, and was beneficial to the company, to the community and to my colleagues too.

When I shared the final version with my manager, she invited me to present the plan to the full Plant leadership council, who gave me full support, allocated the needed budget to the project, and asked me to share a progress report during the next committee meeting. This was a huge and unexpected accelerator, which added a whole new level of commitment -and pressure- to make the second iteration happen as fast as possible.

- So, you have burned the ships, in a way?

- Indeed. And despite having received all the needed support, I still acted on your recommendation to design a Fun system for executing and tracking the progress. I felt that its impact was much appreciated, especially that I didn't have to.

Together with my new team, we designed a logo, chose an inspiring name for our mission, agreed on the milestones to reach, on badges of honor to distribute for each major achievement. With my boss and HR, we also aligned on a new reward and recognition system, in line with company practices, for the major contributions. We did that in a way that would foster collaboration and even some healthy competition.

- Impressive, Sarah! Have your team operations started already?

- Yes, we started 2 weeks ago, and I expect the first results to materialize within next month.

- Next time, we can discuss the 3rd iteration.

- I'll be looking forward to it. Thank you, Mark!"

36

Chapter 6

When Sarah met Mark the following month, she had significantly progressed on her project.

She was pleased to see the level of engagement of her team, which, instead of decreasing with time, actually went the opposite way.

- Would you know what is driving this engagement up?

- The gamification is helping for sure. But more importantly, our early results were reported to the Plant leadership council, and each team member was recognized for their contribution.

- So, can we say you are sharing the credits, and helping your team members to shine?

- Well, yes.

- And would it be true to say that you are earning your team members' respect and further Trust, by behaving as a Servant leader?

- I guess it would be true.

- Great! So, obviously, all the needed enabling habits and personal traits are kicking in at the same time.

- You are so right … as usual!

- Now what?

- There are many months of hard work ahead of us, possibly until the end of the year; yet, I am confident we will get there, based on the progress and results of these first six weeks.

- Well, then this is the right moment to start designing for your third iteration. But first, where do you stand regarding your initial objective?

- My objective of self-fulfillment and self-realization? If it were not for your method, I would say I have already reached my destination: I am delivering more impactful results, I am being largely recognized, and for the first time ever, I am significantly changing the lives of many of my community members! Ally, my manager, even hinted that I am on the right track for another promotion and more responsibilities. So, I can say you have changed my life for the better, Mark!

- Awesome! And I admit that few of my students have reached where you are now, Sarah; and an even fewer number ventured further. So, if you feel like stopping here, I would perfectly understand.

- Wait, no! If you remember, my real aim was to reach my fullest potential, in a way that leaves me with no regrets later. So, yes, I am willing and ready to push further.

You had warned me that each iteration will take me out of my comfort zone; so, considering how much I grew so far, and how much I am enjoying the new me, I am thrilled and filled with expectations about the 3rd iteration. I am absolutely willing to try it if you see me fit for it!

- You definitely are, my friend! Do you remember what the third iteration is?

- Yes: "**Conquer 1+ Level Up**".

40

Chapter 7

- This time around, I want you to meet two people, who best illustrate this third iteration. We will go back to theory afterward.

- Are these two of your students, as you called them?

- Indeed. One is not far from here, while the other is quite remote, and we will connect with her in a few hours when her working day is over.

- Does she work in the mornings only?

- Not quite. She is just in a different time zone.

- Oh my! I was not suspecting that you had such internationally dispersed students. You will need to tell me more about yourself, Mark.

- Sure, I will do so soon. For now, let me call my first student to check if he can come to meet us here. I had given him a heads up that we may want to meet him around 10."

15 minutes later, a handsome young man in his early 30s joined them at the library.

- Here you are, Philip! Good to see you. Let me introduce you to Sarah, my most recent student.

- Hi Sarah! From what Mark told me on the phone, I was impatient to meet this new rising star.

- Oh, come on ... Nice meeting you, Philip. Mark also told me you are one of his best students ever.

- He is too nice as usual. So, I understand that you are now about to deep dive on Mark's third iteration and that you want to learn how it went for me.

- That's correct; all I know now is that it is about "**Conquering 1+ Level Up**", but I have no more details than this.

Mark intervened:

- Tell us about how you planned for yours, please.

- Sure. First, Sarah, let me tell you that I work in a global financial services powerhouse, with operations in many countries. For years, we suffered from a too high turnover among our junior organization. This huge loss was still considered as acceptable by many as it was pretty much in line with the rest of our industry. To me, this wasn't ok. I couldn't accept to lose a good portion of my best talents every year.

So, in my first iteration, I achieved best-in-class retention rates, thanks to being close to my direct reports and providing them with the needed coaching and genuine care. Later, I expanded this success to the whole subsidiary I work in, by providing hands-on training to all managers of others.

This training integrated people development best practices, and learnings and templates from my personal experience. So, for my third iteration, I had the wild dream to transform all the corporation into a more caring place, with best-in-class retention rates across the industry.

- And how large is your company, if I may ask?

- There are around 18,000 employees in total; 15,000 of them have less than five years of tenure.

- And you wanted to improve their everyday work life all by yourself?

- Well, I knew I couldn't do it by myself. Still, thanks to Mark's inspiration, I believed I could do something about it.

- Interesting! So, how did you solve for it?

- I kind of reverse-engineered the whole thing: to improve the work life of these 15,000 junior colleagues, I needed to train their bosses, so slightly less than 3,000 managers. With 20 people per training, we'd need 150 training sessions, which I could still not deliver on my own; so, I considered training additional trainers to join me.

As a result, with only three train-the-trainer sessions, I could cover the whole company.

- Wait! Three sessions only? So, you formed 60 trainers, who delivered three training sessions each, with 20 managers per session ... that's 3600 training slots. Brilliant! It seems so easy now.

- I would not say easy, rather, doable.

- Right! It gives a solid reason to believe that it can be done.

- Yes, and in a relatively short time.

- So, where is the catch?"

Philip smiled and replied:

"Now that you have seen the bright side, here is a sample of the questions I needed to get ready for:

- How would we fill up the training classrooms?
- Why would managers attend?
- How could we organize all the sessions?
- Would the subsidiaries pay for the expenses?
- How to sustain the same training quality?
- Could I commit upfront to deliver the cumulative retention transformation?
- Had I missed any key ingredients from the two iterations I had delivered myself when designing the third one that will be delivered through others?

- How did you solve for all these questions?

- Well, for a start, I leveraged the first enablers even harder: I connected with as many organization leaders as possible, across subsidiaries, to understand what would get them to join and commit to the program. I also recruited the needed 60 trainers through a TV-show-like selection campaign, which attracted many candidates.

These In touch and Fun activities gave me a solid start.

To sustain the program, I thought harder about building sponsorship at the highest level; so, I stroke a joint deal with both the corporate head of HR and the corporate head of Operations. The first would benefit from the reduced need to hire in replacement for attrition, while the second would enjoy stronger results and less information and client loss, which inevitably happened with every resignation.

- That's smart! Did you identify these partnership opportunities thanks to your in touch activities?

- That is correct! I initially hadn't realized that it was such a pain for both organizations as my starting point was only to help the junior colleagues to thrive.

- Interesting! I bet these partnerships gave you the needed sponsorship.

- Indeed, HR helped with the training logistics and expenses, and Operations mandated that all managers should attend a session within the next six months. On top, they raised the retention expectations on all key managers' scorecards. From my end, I committed to having all the 3,000 managers trained, and supported afterward, as they attempted to apply the learnings in their day-to-day work.

- Wow! Awesome! And where have you reached so far?

- Oh, this program was executed last year and has slightly exceeded the expectations. I dare to say it contributed to our company being in last year 'best companies to work for' shortlist and realizing a jump in both client retention and profitability.

- Philip, this is impressive! So, what would be your advice, as I get ready to kick off my third iteration?

- From my experience, looking for Leverage made a big difference: Given the wide reach, I needed to work on my capabilities to build partnerships and strike deals, and on my abilities to attract others to join the mission freely.

Mark had also made me realize that I had a natural tendency to Be Results oriented. And I agree as I couldn't afford to dilute my efforts in non-result generating activities. Given the scale and the pressure on timing, I couldn't have succeeded otherwise.

- How did this Results orientation materialize?

- Well, I would say the reverse-engineering helped me to list exactly the actions that were necessary to reach my goal -and nothing more- and the effective decomposition led to a reasonable pyramid of effort.

- An effective decomposition? Do you mean how you worked the numbers back from 15,000 people in your target group, to 3,000 managers, to 150 sessions, to 60 trainers to be trained in 3 sessions?

- Correct, in three well-calculated rounds, we could reach all the organization.

- Thank you so much, Philip! I understand why Mark advised to learn the third iteration from you. Your success story is a great inspiration, and I am making many mental notes for reapplication.

- Happy to help, Sarah! Let me know if you need help as you go through your third iteration.

- I will. Thank you very much for offering!

Chapter 8

After Philip left, Sarah was deep in her thoughts; she had learned so much through his experience.

All of which made sense, and most could be applied directly to her case.

Mark observed her in silence, giving her as much time as she needed.

After a while, Sarah noticed the silence and apologized.

- No problem at all. Shall we have tea or coffee at the cafeteria before we call my next student? It will be more convenient to contact her from there than from within the library.

- Sure, a cup of tea would be welcome!"

Mark shared additional background on his other student:

- We will soon call Aicha, my North African student. After she graduated from university with a Ph.D., she launched a successful startup in technology.

Two years later, she felt an urge to give back to her community; so, she returned to her country, established an office in a deep rural area, and is vowing to help women to start their own flourishing business.

- This is quite inspiring.

- Wait until you hear more from her. You will be even more inspired.

Thirty minutes later, they connected over a voice and video call with Aicha.

- Hi Mark! What a pleasure to see you again.

- Same pleasure here, Aicha. Thank you for making the time. Let me please introduce Sarah.

- Hi, Sarah, how are you? By now, you already met Philip, right?

- Hi Aicha, yes, I have, and I am looking forward to also learning from you.

- Of course! My dream is to make a difference for my country, especially for the people who need it the most. I believe that, with a proper design, I can change people's lives and leave a mark at a macro-level.

I wanted to start from the poorest and most secluded area, so I opted for a small village lodged high in the mountains. For two months, I lived there to understand the villagers' situation, constraints, and aspirations. This helped me to uncover many of their strengths, so I could propose them with a plan to commercialize their local specialties, leveraging my connections abroad.

Building on the small-scale success, I expanded to 10 villages from the neighborhood, to whom I was warmly recommended by the pilot village leader. This worked very well, so the regional district authorities asked if I could further expand the program to all the hundred villages in their geography. This would help over 40,000 households, and hence 200,000 people, get out of poverty.

The first villagers shared their experience during a roadshow to build the Trust needed to start the program. To allow each household to make at least 5 dollars per day would require us to reach 200 thousand dollars of sales per day, and around 73 million dollars per year, which required more capabilities in logistics, sales, IT, and marketing.

The district authorities gladly agreed to avail a central warehouse; we also sought and obtained national and UN funds supporting women-led businesses, to get ready on all other aspects. On the commercial side, I approached one of the leading international retail chains, who promoted fair trade and organic products and were looking for a differentiation versus competitors; we negotiated a 10-year exclusive distribution agreement against a commitment to purchase up to $100 million per year of the villages' production.

One year after we started, we have exceeded our targets, and the testimonials I regularly receive fill me with joy and pride, as I see our contribution to improving my fellow citizens' lives.

Worth mentioning, the program received many national and international awards, and I am regularly invited to share our experience in international forums.

- Do you know what your next mission will be, now that you have finished?

- Finished? I have just started! Remember that my vision is to impact the whole country. I am now in discussions with the national program for poverty eradication to design a nation-wide proposal, and I also received requests from other African countries to reapply. You see, I am not quite done yet.

- This is <u>Results orientation</u> and <u>Leverage</u> at their best!

- Thank you! Mark had helped me to refine my strategy and make it as big as possible. His method, followed to the letter, does marvels.

Mark replied:

- It is you, dear Aicha, who did marvels. You are also a source of inspiration, as I see the efforts you invest to help others in getting a better future, and the energy you derive from doing so.

- My biggest pleasure. Anyway, Sarah, if you need further details, just let me know, and I will happily oblige.

- Thank you again Aicha for sharing; this is such a wonderful inspiration.

Chapter 9

'So, what have you learned today about the third iteration?

- It targets a whole new level versus the previous ones. If the first iteration happens in a pond and the second iteration happens in a lake, the third takes place in an ocean! It is as if they were only prototypes to learn from and to finetune the final undertaking.

- Excellent! What else?

- Given the large scale, the design includes a perfectly oiled structure, including a central enabling group; for Philip, it was the training logistics group, and for Aicha, it was the central warehouse and the commercialization contracts. Reinforcing the processes, selecting the right people, preparing the sponsorship, and simplifying the mission with focused tasks and ready-for-use templates is kind of building the needed ship to sail on the above ocean.

From the perspective of any contributing resource, the ask is therefore simplified to the minimum, e.g., each trainer delivers 3 training sessions only. And yet, collectively, they will change the world.

- Absolutely correct!

- In both examples, they built synergies with other organizations to act as acceleration sponsors. Was this a coincidence, or part of your method?

- It is indeed an essential component. As Philip stated, building <u>Leverage</u> is the enabling habit of the third iteration, and it makes all the difference between successful undertakings and transformation attempts that take years without reaching their full potential.

- Noted!

- In between <u>Fun</u> and <u>Results orientation</u>, you can assign time-bound deliverables to each sub-team and create some soft dependencies between these teams to generate an emulation between the most engaged groups and the laggards. Also, build your plans with some extra capacity, to account for some positive or negative variance.

- Oh, so this is why Philip made plans for 3,600 training slots while he had less than 3,000 managers to train, and why Aicha signed a contract up to $100 million per year while she only needed $73 million per year to achieve her objectives!

- Yes, you make solid plans, and you stay ready to update them at every milestone, as needed.

- Would you have some additional advice for me?

- Sure, given your second iteration is on track, it is time to prepare your grand vision for the third iteration and to design a proper activities system for it. You may need to refine your plan many times, so it's good to start now.

Also, as you identify the potential acceleration sponsors, it would be good to involve them in some simple way in your second iteration, this will make it easier to embark them with you when you reach your third iteration.

- And this way, if they are not very responsive, I will know that I can't count on them later and would refine my plans as you said, early enough

- That's also correct!

- I have another question, please: what does the "1+" mean, in the third iteration?

- It means that there are many levels above your area of belonging, and it's up to you to choose the one you want to play at. Regardless of which one you choose, you will end up delivering way more than you thought yourself to be capable of.

- Can you please illustrate?

- Sure! In your current mission, you could choose your third iteration to impact the plants in your company that manufacture the same products as yours, or all plants regardless of their product lines, or even all manufacturing companies in your industry. So, see? There are many possible levels to contribute to. You can even keep iterating, each time growing by one level.

- Then, how shall I choose the right level? Would you recommend any criteria to do so?

- It all depends on your passion ... and on the time and energy you want to dedicate to the third iteration; obviously, the higher the level, the longer it will take to reach there.

If your time or your passion is low, I would advise to stop at the second iteration. That would still be an achievement you can be proud of. If both time and passion are high, you -for sure- won't settle for anything less than the maximum possible. If either time or passion is medium, a smart way is to check first how much leverage you can get, and then settle your level based on that.

Mark took a small piece of paper and drew below diagram on it for illustration:

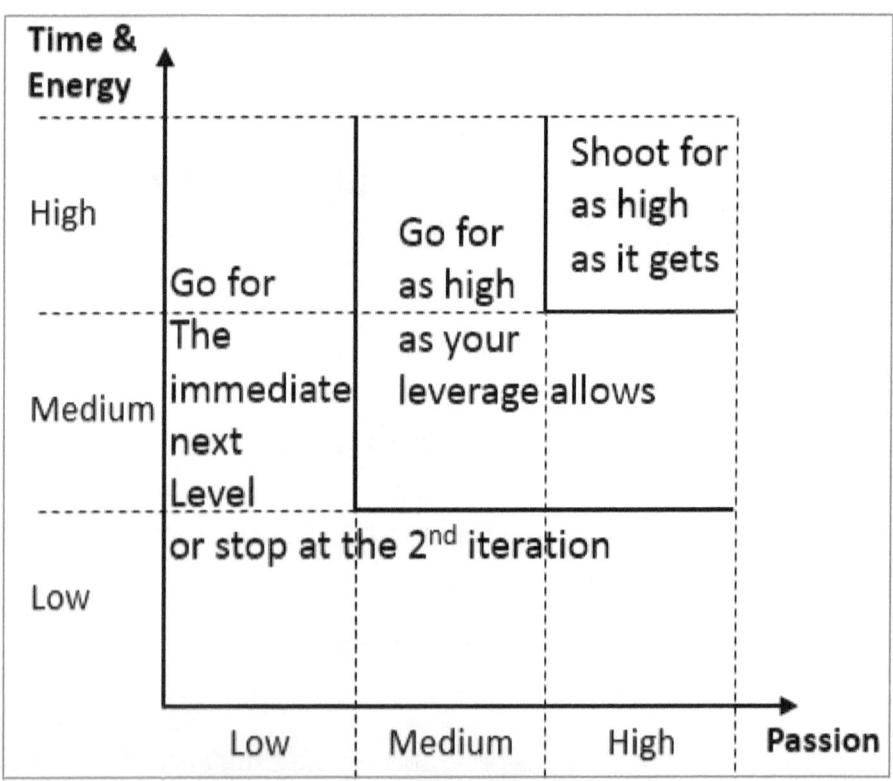

- I see! Anything else before I get started?

- Yes, did you notice how Philip and Aicha's plans seemed deceivingly simple?

- True! I was wondering why others hadn't already executed them before.

- Well, it takes a good blend of <u>Being in touch</u>, experience, and passion to understand how the various links of the system connect to each other and to determine the most effective way to reach your destination and avoid pitfalls that are invisible to the neophyte.

- So, this is why you advised me to pick an area I am good at, and for which I have passion, right? So that I already have two of the three ingredients of this magic blend?

- That's a smart remark, and it is obviously paying out well for you so far.

- Thank you, Mark, for the advice and the encouragement. I feel ready to start my design."

3rd Iteration Instructions

- Choose the suitable level to target.
- Draft a head-turning vision statement.
- <Optional> Design the execution pyramid.
- Design the activities system including a tracking system.
- Identify a Leverage and lock partnerships.
- Be in touch at 360°, with the sponsors, the contributors & the beneficiaries.
- Involve key resources & sponsors in the 2nd iteration, at least in the communication.
- Finalize the objective & the head-turning vision statement.
- Execute with excellence.

58

Chapter 10

In their next encounter, Mark asked Sarah if she would share her story with some of his future students.

"Sure, I would! When would you want me to?

- Let's say early next year, once you have made solid inroads in your third iteration.

- Fair enough. So, this is what you do? Build a pyramid of World Changers where one generation inspires the next?

- Yes, this is my current mission: to build a sustained thread of individuals who will make a significant positive impact.

- Wouldn't this be a fourth iteration?

- Hahaha! Yes, kind of.

- How did the whole thing start?

- Several years ago, I formalized the method, after I noticed that I naturally operated in this manner and that I usually achieved more, even when I hadn't much authority.

Each cycle of three iterations would reinforce my equity and my network of supporters, many of whom volunteered to contribute when I launched subsequent endeavors. So, year after year, making meaningful and more complex changes became easier. After some time, I envisioned what you called my fourth iteration, to spread the method and build a network of people who can change the world for the better.

- Is your volunteering in the library part of it?

- In part yes. As I serve in the 'people development' section, it helps me to stay in touch, and now and then, meet young promising people like yourself. It is also time well spent to meditate and think about my plans.

- Interesting! So, when does your quest to change the world end?

- In essence, it is a way of thinking; so, it applies to all things you undertake. Whatever matters to you, you can make it better and more impactful.

- Does it work for everyone?

- Most people have at least one passion area for which they'd be ready to go the extra mile. Some need to try many experiences to find theirs. Eventually, everyone will be interested. Whether the method will work for all, from my experience with my students, some will be happy with the first two iterations, while others will go all the way till the third one.

Also, remember that the supporting personal character traits can't be faked and will take time to nurture; their level of maturity will be the key differentiating factor between successful and very successful applications.

- One last thing, I feel I could launch a couple of applications in parallel; would you advise against it?

- Of course, you can! As long as one doesn't happen at the expense of the other. As you start, you will benefit from focusing on one application at a time; and later, when you master the method, you could have two or even three applications running in parallel, possibly in different stages."

Mark and Sarah agreed to meet quarterly thereafter; and this was very beneficial for Sarah as she completed her third iteration plans, identified sponsors for the leverage she needed and successfully closed her second iteration within 1 year.

The first 2 months had been mainly focused on planning activities, then the implementation started.

Sarah brought in the company's country public relations expert to lead the collaboration with the city's mayor to scale the program up and select and train 100 young entrepreneurs who would buy and resell the unneeded finished products from the 30 production lines.

Internally, Ally, the plant manager, agreed to the creation of a "finished products valorization" position within the logistics department, to manage the collection, storage, and shipment operations for this new line of business, and the finance department agreed on special commercial conditions to defer payments for 90 days for the first 2 years as additional support for the new entrepreneurs. These activity system interventions moved the transformation from its project status to become a sustainable ongoing operation.

By the end of the year, the plant had reduced its recycling expenses, increased its revenue and, most importantly, achieved its goal of zero solid waste to landfill 4 years ahead of the total company's deadline.

As Ally shared this impressive achievement in her yearly plant newsletter to the company's CEO, she and Sarah were invited to the head office to present this program to the company's executives at their next monthly meeting.

For Sarah, this was huge: her first intercontinental business trip, her first visit to the company head office, and her first meeting with the CEO or with any of his lead team members.

Alan, the CEO [1], warmly welcomed Ally and Sarah:

(1) *See "The EPIC Manager", from the same author.*

- So, Ally, this is your protege?

- Yes, Alan, Sarah is the mastermind behind this transformation.

- Nice to meet you, Sarah. Ally has been very complimentary about your passion and leadership. I am happy to finally meet you in person.

- I'm honored to be here!

- Your program has caught our attention because we want to strengthen the company's environmental commitment with innovative programs. We were impressed with the simplicity of the design, the flawless execution, and the groundbreaking results that you achieved. Do you think you could reapply your project to all the other plants? You could do so remotely or from here if you are willing to relocate temporarily. I would personally sponsor this global program and avail the needed resources.

Sarah was speechless; she had come prepared with data to try to convince the executive committee to support her 3rd iteration, and here she is, being offered everything she had hoped for. Her strong results had obviously done the job on her behalf.

She immediately accepted the offer and, as she had learned from Ally [2], she took 5 minutes to ask Allan a few more questions about scope, firm and stretch goals, expected milestones, target dates, executives involved, method to communicate with him if necessary.

[2] *See "The EPIC Manager", from the same author.*

Six months later, she was further promoted, as the executive committee members were delighted with her results and recognized her potential for continued growth.

She noticed that this three-iteration method had become a way of thinking, as Mark had predicted: when faced with lofty goals, she would turn them from topics of concern to topics of influence, one iteration at a time, addressing them first on a smaller scale, before attempting to resolve them completely.

She was also immensely pleased and humbled when Mark called her to share her experience with some of his newest students the following year.

As she reflected, she was amazed by the personal growth she had achieved, and she knew this was just the beginning.

"I am on the right path to reach the success I deserve, and to leave a legacy ... Wait for me World, I'm coming!"

The End

Change the World in 3 Iterations

The 3 Iterations,

The 3 Supporting Personal Characters Traits,

& The 3 Enabling Habits

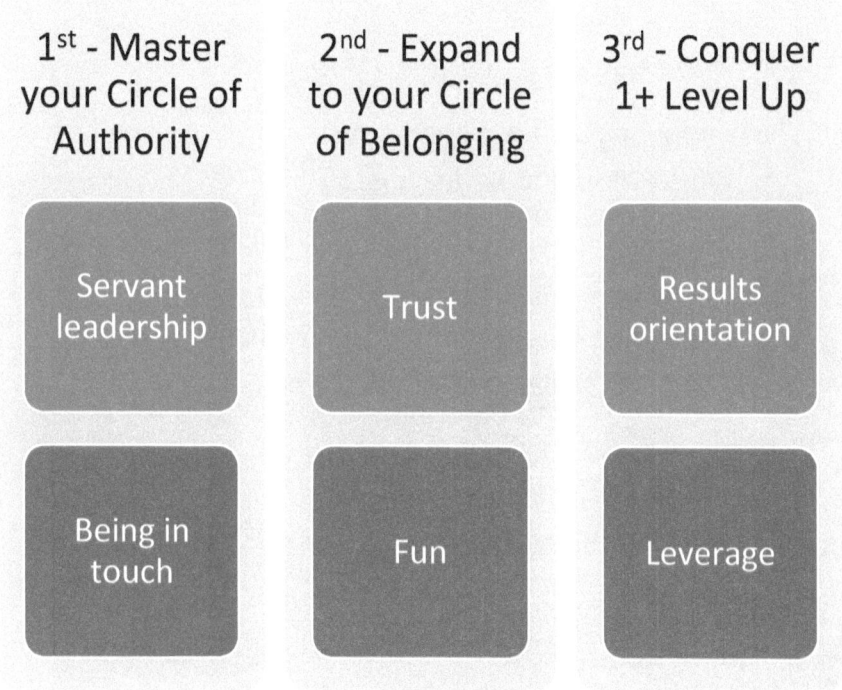

Dear Reader,

I hope you enjoyed reading this book!

Thank you for your time and let me wish you all the best in your World-changing endeavors!

If you have any comment or question, or want to share how you applied the 3-iteration method to change the world, please don't hesitate to reach out to me.

I'd be grateful if you could leave a Review on https://www.amazon.com/dp/1794387080, to help others discover the book.

Soufiane Erraji

soufiane.erraji.author@gmail.com

From the same author

"Radical Transformation" Trilogy - Volume 1

"The Breakthrough Organization" is a business book that follows the journey of a new CEO tasked with rescuing a troubled company.

Will he succeed to turn the situation around, restore profitability and turn the company into a best place to work, despite the challenges and betrayals?

Behind the story, this is a book of strong leadership, communication, and company culture. The CEO's journey serves as a guide for leaders seeking to transform their own organizations into profitable and rewarding places to work.

Available in paper and e-book on https://www.amazon.com/dp/B0BYG5M3KL

From the same author

"Radical Transformation" Trilogy - Volume 2

"The EPIC ™ Manager" book offers a time-tested framework, to transform the manager-report relationship.

Managers will discover a step-by-step approach to be highly successful through building their organization.

All readers will find out how to own their destiny by being proactive in managing their managers.

Together, they will learn how to reach success through interdependence.

Available in paper, e-book, and audiobook formats on **Amazon**.

About the author

Soufiane Erraji specializes in organization excellence. He has 27 years of experience as IT director & master coach at a Fortune-50 company, leading teams in Europe, Asia, and Africa.

He is an author, speaker, and mentor to professionals from various countries, businesses, and industries.

His qualities as a manager, coach, and trainer have earned him numerous awards in the fields of training and personal development.

He is also a visiting professor at Ecole Centrale de Casablanca. His books have been read in 60 countries, and his conferences have been attended by thousands of people from 30 countries.

soufiane.erraji.author@gmail.com

www.linkedin.com/in/soufiane-erraji-03b4512/

This is a work of fiction. Names, characters, business, events, and incidents are the products of the author's imagination. Any resemblance to actual persons, living or dead, or actual events is purely coincidental.

Copyright © Soufiane Erraji, 2019

Legal Deposit: 2019 MO 0467

All rights reserved, including the right of reproduction or transmission in whole or in part in any form or by any means, electronic or mechanical, without express written permission from Soufiane Erraji

soufiane.erraji.author@gmail.com

www.ingramcontent.com/pod-product-compliance
Lightning Source LLC
Chambersburg PA
CBHW021501210526
45463CB00002B/843